The Gift Of

The Word Of

Wisdom

D0840677

by

Norvel Hayes

(Volume number two of a nine part series on The Gifts Of The Spirit.)

HARRISON HOUSE
P.O. Box 35035
Tulsa, Okla. 74135

(All Scripture quotations in this volume are from *The King James Version* of the Bible, unless otherwise stated.)

"For to one is given by the Spirit the word of wisdom . . ." (I Corinthians 12:8).

ISBN 0-89274-140-6
Copyright © 1979 by Norvel Hayes
Printed in the United States of America
All Rights Reserved

Table of Contents

Chapter 1
The Gift Of The Word Of Wisdom: What Is It? 5

Chapter 2
The Gift Of The Word Of Wisdom: Who Needs It? 9

Chapter 3
God Gave The Word Of Wisdom To
Old Testament Men 13

Chapter 4
Paul And A Word of God's Wisdom 15

Chapter 5
God's Word Of Wisdom Came Through An Angel 17

Chapter 6
You Need God's Word Of Wisdom..................... 19

Chapter 7
God Gave Me A Vision............................... 25

Chapter 8
Stand Steadfast................................... 33

1

The Gift Of The Word Of Wisdom: What Is It?

Are you living in the spirit? Unless you study the Bible, and base a lot of your existing (a lot of your living, and a lot of your talking) upon the Word of God, and the ways of God, you are not living in the spirit. You are living in the natural.

That was the problem with some of the members of the church at Corinth. In chapters four and five of the book of 1 Corinthians, Paul wrote, "I don't like some of the things that you have been doing. Some of you are eating too much, and you are going to mess yourselves up if you do that." He said, "Besides that, you are allowing one of your men down there to live with a woman that he is not supposed to be living with. You are going to have to get rid of him. He can't be a spiritual leader in the church and do that."

Paul also said, "Some of you are going around saying that you have God's power. Well, I can't tell if you do or not, because of the way some of you are living and acting. But, I am going to come and see you as soon as the Lord will let me, and when I get there, I shall find out just how much of God's power you have." He said, "God's power is not something that you get up and brag about. If you have God's power you are living by it" (Author's paraphrase).

God's power is living. You live that way. You watch what you say to other people. You don't cut them down or drag them down. You always try to help somebody, or to build them up. You don't push people into the gutter: the devil is in that kind of business.

If you have been born again by the Spirit of God, you are supposed to be helping Jesus, and not the devil. God loves the human race, so don't you help the devil.

Many Christians that I meet, talk and act as though they are representing the devil. I just want to buy them a "devil button" and let them wear it, because they are not representing Jesus. They think that they are representing Jesus because they go to a good meeting, or to church where He is manifesting himself so sweetly, and they get blessed. Then when they get home, they act like the devil himself.

You live by God's power. You don't just say, "I get blessed at church, therefore I am living by His power."

When you are trying to live by God's power, the Holy Ghost will give you everything; not part of the things, but everything you need. He will teach you or show you all things.

In this particular volume, on the gifts of the Spirit, we are going to take a closer look at the gift of the word of wisdom. We will begin by reading verse one of the 12th chapter of I Corinthians. "Now concerning spiritual gifts, brethren, I would not have you ignorant." Remember, this gift is no different from the "gifts of healing," or any of the rest of the gifts of the Spirit. God does not want you ignorant concerning *the word of wisdom.* As you learn the meaning of *the gift of the word of wisdom,* and how badly you need it, you will find how exciting that it can be in your own life.

Paul says in verse 8: "For to one is given by the Spirit the word of wisdom . . . ." What does he mean?

The *gift of the word of wisdom* is a "word of God's knowledge of what is going to take place." It is not what is taking place right now. I am not talking about that. We

6

will study the *gift of the word of knowledge* in another volume in this series on the gifts of the Spirit. The *gift of the word of wisdom* is **the divine revelation of God that tells or shows what is going to take place.**

2

The Gift Of The Word Of Wisdom: Who Needs It?

You may say, "Why do I need *the gift of the word of wisdom?*"

Whether or not you are involved in *the gift of the word of wisdom* yourself, depends upon whether you—as a Christian, yield yourself to God. If you yield yourself to Him, it will come to pass. The Holy Ghost will manifest himself and tell you that it is God's will for you to receive *the gift of the word of wisdom.* He will tell you what is God's will for you in the future, or what is going to take place. It is a word of God's knowledge when He tells human beings what is going to take place in the future. It is given to you by the Holy Ghost—supernaturally manifesting himself to you. And God doesn't want you to be ignorant of that.

Let's read 1 Corinthians 12, beginning with verse 1, again, and see what Paul has to say about the spiritual gifts. "Now concerning spiritual gifts, brethren, I would not have you ignorant. Ye know that ye were Gentiles, carried away unto these dumb idols, even as ye were led. Wherefore I give you to understand, that no man speaking by the Spirit of God calleth Jesus accursed: and that no man can say that Jesus is the Lord, but by the Holy Ghost. Now there are diversities of gifts, but the same Spirit. And there are differences of administrations, but the same Lord. And there are diversities of operations, but it is the same God which worketh all in all. But the manifestation of the Spirit is given to every man to profit withal" (vv. 1-7).

The manifestation of the Spirit for the *word of wisdom* is badly needed. In fact, all of the *gifts of the Spirit* are important. Each *gift of the Spirit* has its place. One cannot take the place of the other. Each one of them has its own distinct way of helping you, during your life here on the earth. And each gift is given by the Holy Ghost. We just read in verse 7, that "the manifestation of the Spirit is given to every man to profit withal."

The *word of wisdom* is given to you for your own private life. It is given to you to help you. Verse 8 says, "For to one is given by the Spirit the word of wisdom . . . ."

Many times, the *word of wisdom* will operate through a person, to an individual or to a group of people in public assembly. Most Christians never have that operating in their life, unless they are called into the public ministry. But all Christians can have *the word of wisdom* operating in their lives for themselves. They can have that same gift to operate in their own personal lives, and also to help their friends. It works the same way.

"For to one is given by the Spirit the word of wisdom; to another the word of knowledge by the same Spirit; To another faith by the same Spirit; to another the gifts of healing by the same Spirit; To another the working of miracles; to another prophecy; to another discerning of spirits; to another divers kinds of tongues; to another the interpretation of tongues: But all these worketh that one and the selfsame Spirit, dividing to every man severally as he will. For as the body is one, and hath many members, and all the members of that one body, being many, are one body: so also is Christ" (vv. 8-12). We will drop down to the 18th verse: it picks up about the body again. *"But now hath God set the members every one of them in the body, as it hath pleased him."*

You see, we are supposed to be so close together, just as the parts of the human body are joined together. When we are born again, we become members of the Body of Christ. We are brothers and sisters in Christ, and we are supposed to be absolutely in love with each other. God has set the members in the Body of Christ exactly where He wants them.

"And if they were all one member, where were the body? But now are they many members, yet but one body. And the eye cannot say unto the hand, I have no need of thee: nor again the head to the feet, I have no need of you" (vv. 19-21).

You can't look over to the person next to you, and say, "Well, I have no need of you. I have been making it all these years without you. I don't even know you, and I don't need you." You need them! You need their love.

Ten years from now, they may move next door to you. And sometime when you are in trouble, the Holy Ghost may give them *a word of wisdom* for you; to tell you something that is going to happen to you in the future. They can walk over to your house, and knock on your door, and say, "Oh! I've got to talk to you! The Lord told me something that is going to happen to you . . . . He showed me in a vision . . . ."

That is how God gets His knowledge over to the human race. He is the supernatural God—the spiritual God, and we are natural people. God gives *His word of wisdom* to us through the power of the Holy Ghost who is within us.

You need the spiritual *gift of the word of wisdom*, working in your life.

11

3

God Gave The Word Of Wisdom To Old Testament Men

Back in Old Testament times, most all of the old prophets had *the word of wisdom* operating in their lives, to show them what was going to happen in the future. In fact, the prophet Elisha told the children of Israel all about their enemies. He told them what their enemies were going to do, and what they could do about it. (See 2 Kings 6:8-12.)

Of course, the Syrians wanted to kill Elisha. They said, "Let's kill him. We had better get him out of the way. We can't win a war like that." And they couldn't. *The word of wisdom* was working for Israel, and it made no difference if Syria had a hundred thousand soldiers, and the other side had only a thousand, *the word of wisdom* worked by the Spirit, and told Elisha what was going to happen. And Elisha told the children of Israel.

The *word of wisdom* not only tells you what is going to happen to you in the future, but it will also tell you what God's will is for you in the future.

God gave *a word of wisdom* to Noah. And I believe that when I receive something about an individual, it is the same identical gift that God gave to Noah. I believe that Noah actually received *a word of wisdom* from God on the earth.

God manifested himself to Noah in the 6th chapter of Genesis. He told Noah, in detail, how to build an ark. He told Noah that it was going to rain.

It didn't rain for over a hundred years, but God told Noah that something was going to happen in the future. Notice, beginning with verse 11: "The earth also was corrupt before God, and the earth was filled with violence. And God looked upon the earth, and, behold, it was corrupt; for all flesh had corrupted his way upon the earth. And God said unto Noah, The end of all flesh is come before me; for the earth is filled with violence through them; and, behold, I will destroy them with the earth" (vv. 11-13).

God then said, in verses 14, and 15; "Make thee an ark of gopher wood; rooms shalt thou make in the ark, and shalt pitch it within and without with pitch. And this is the fashion which thou shalt make it of . . . ." God went on to tell Noah how to build the ark, and what to put on the ark. Noah received that *word of wisdom* from God, and eight people were saved to replenish the earth, as well as every species of animal—"all that in whose nostrils was the breath of life."

4

Paul And A Word of God's Wisdom

We now go to the New Testament for a look at God's *gift of the word of wisdom* at work. A prime example of someone who availed himself of the gift of *the word of wisdom* was Paul. Paul received *a word of God's wisdom* when they were conspiring to massacre him. Paul had been preaching the gospel, and he had just been rescued from the angry mob. It looked as though there was no hope. There were more than forty men who said, "I am going to eat nothing, and drink nothing, until Paul dies!" Now that is pretty strong. It is bad enough to have two or three men after you to kill you, but when all the leaders say that you are going to die, and forty men say that they aren't going to eat or drink until you are dead, that is serious.

From the natural, how in the world could Paul know what was God's will? Paul was a human being, just like you and me. He didn't know everything in the natural. But, Paul had the Holy Ghost living within him. The only thing that Paul knew more than you, is what the Holy Ghost gave him through *the word of wisdom.* Paul wrote over half of the New Testament because the Holy Ghost came upon him. The Holy Ghost wrote the New Testament through Paul and others. He gave to them great *words of wisdom.*

We read in Acts 23:11; "And the night following the Lord stood by him, and said, Be of good cheer, Paul: for as thou hast testified of me in Jerusalem, so must thou bear witness also at Rome." That is all that Paul needed!

Paul said (in other words) "I am not going to die. It doesn't make any difference how many people are fasting for my death. It doesn't make any difference how many leaders say that they are going to kill me. I don't care how many jails that I am in, or how much blood is running off me, or how badly they beat me! Oh, thank God! I am going to preach at Rome! because God said that I am to be of good cheer. As I have testified of Him in Jerusalem, so must I bear witness in Rome!"

If you read the life of Paul, you will find that he always wanted to go to Rome and preach. So he said, "Before I die — before I leave this earth, I am going to preach at Rome. God said so, and that is the way it is!

The gift of the word of wisdom worked through Paul.

5

God's Word Of Wisdom Came Through An Angel

God can use you to give yourself *a word of wisdom* through the Holy Ghost that is within you. He can use another person to give you *the word of wisdom*, and He can use angels. Such was the case with Cornelius. He sent an angel to Cornelius' house to tell him what to do, and whom to talk to, and what would happen to him if he would obey God. Cornelius wasn't even saved, although he was praying. But God heard Cornelius' prayer coming up to the throne.

Many people pray, yet they are not saved. They believe that Jesus is real. They have great respect for God. But nobody has ever taken the time to tell them how to get saved. They only have a kind of vague intellectual vision of God, and Jesus. They have a great respect for Him, but as far as being born again, or having an experience with the Spirit of the living God, they have never done so.

Cornelius was that type of person. He had a good heart about him, but he was not born again. You can read about Cornelius' experience in the 10th chapter of the book of Acts. I will paraphrase it. Cornelius had been praying up to the throne of God, and the Holy Ghost showed Cornelius what to do. An angel appeared unto him and said, "You send some men down to Joppa. There is a man down there." You see, God knew that Cornelius wanted to be saved, but he didn't know how. The angel told Cornelius, "There is a man there by the name of Peter, living in a certain house. So, send some men down there and tell Peter to come up here, and he will give you the words whereby you and your household shall be saved." That was a point of *God's knowledge through a word of wisdom from God*, as to what was going to happen in the future. Cornelius had a part to play, just as many times, an individual has a part to play if something is to come to pass or not.

The word of wisdom is not the same as *the word of knowledge. The word of wisdom* points to the future, as to what is going to happen. And *the word of God's knowledge* is what is happening right now—not next week—but right now.

The word of God's knowledge is like a lawyer with a vast storehouse of knowledge. God gives a little of His wisdom to show you how to do a certain thing. Wisdom and knowledge work very close together. God imparts His wisdom: wisdom to know how to do things. You have to know how to do things, therefore you have to listen to God. You can't get ahead of Him. The manifestation of God brings to you a word—not God's whole wisdom, but *a word of wisdom. A word of wisdom* to you is just a small fragment of God's mind, of the will of God, for you, and the purpose of God for you on the earth. Not the whole—just a small part. That is the reason God has listed it as "a word of wisdom." You don't get very much of it at a time: just a little bit.

The angel could not tell Cornelius how to get saved, but he, through the Holy Ghost using him, could tell Cornelius who to go to for the information on how to get saved. Cornelius did as the angel told him; he sent men down to Joppa, and they brought Peter back with them, because the Spirit of God had been working on Peter also. Peter obeyed the Spirit of God, and as a result, Cornelius and his entire household was saved when the Holy Ghost fell on them.

6

You Need God's Word Of Wisdom

It is when God gives you *the word of His wisdom to* use: to let you know what is going on, or what is to take place in the future, that you can talk about being successful in your undertakings. Through *the word of His wisdom* you can find out exactly what you need in your daily life, and exactly the way the situation is.

The entire second chapter of 1 Corinthians concerns the revelation of God to man: *the word of wisdom,* etc.

"And I, brethren, when I came to you, came not with excellency of speech or wisdom, declaring unto you the testimony of God.

For I determined not to know any thing among you, save Jesus Christ, and him crucified.

And I was with you in weakness, and in fear, and in much trembling.

And my speech and my preaching was not with enticing words of man's wisdom, but in demonstration of the Spirit and of power:

That your faith should not stand in the wisdom of men, but in the power of God.

Howbeit we speak wisdom among them that are perfect: yet not the wisdom of this world, nor of the princes of this world, that come to nought:

But we speak the wisdom of God in a mystery, even the hidden wisdom, which God ordained before the world unto our glory" (vv. 1-7).

I would like to emphasize verse 7: "But we speak the wisdom of God in a mystery, even the hidden wisdom, which God ordained before the world unto our glory." Please study that verse! You can get a glimpse of God's love for you in there. God wants to give you His mind.

"Which none of the princes of this world knew: for had they known it, they would not have crucified the Lord of glory. But as it is written, Eye hath not seen, nor ear heard, neither have entered into the heart of man, the things which God hath prepared for them that love him. But God hath revealed them unto us by his Spirit: for the Spirit searcheth all things, yea, the deep things of God" (vv. 8-10).

Please understand: they are revealed to us by God's Spirit.

"For what man knoweth the things of a man, save the spirit of man which is in him? even so the things of God knoweth no man, but the Spirit of God" (v. 11).

You cannot get God's ideas on things unless the Holy Ghost gives them to you. The Holy Ghost knows the mind of God: you do not. If you want to know the real truth about anything, you have to get it from the Spirit of God who lives inside you.

Have you ever heard anybody say, "Well, I thought that it was the Lord's will. But boy! it must not have been. This is a mess! I'm not sure it is the Lord's will for me to get married to him."

Well! If things are a mess, it was not the Lord's will. It was your will. You decided that. The Holy Ghost did not tell you to do it. In fact, that is the problem with most American homes today. God didn't have anything to do with putting over half of the marriages together. The

20

Holy Ghost did not put most husbands and wives together. They put themselves together. They will say, "I like the way she is built. Oh, I wouldn't mind her!"

If you are a man, it is good to like pretty girls, but you shouldn't go around marrying one, just because she is pretty. That pretty girl may not be the one that God has planned for you. You have to find out from God, who He wants you to marry.

"Now we have received, not the spirit of the world, but the spirit which is of God; that we might know the things that are freely given to us of God" (v. 12).

I have been telling Jesus, "Jesus, do you want to send me a wife? Just go ahead and freely send her. If you don't have any sweet little angels, forget it! Lord, deliver me from messes!" If you pray much, like that, you may not marry at all!

If you married a man or woman simply because he or she was pretty, or for their looks, you may be in a mess. And you may be saying, "Lord, how did I get into this mess?" We need to know that the things that are freely given to us come from the Lord. And we do this by allowing our spirit man to listen to the Spirit of God, as He gives us *the word of wisdom:* to know what is to come in our lives.

"Which things also we speak, not in the words which man's wisdom teacheth, but which the Holy Ghost teacheth; comparing spiritual things with spiritual" (v. 13).

That is where people get mixed up. We should not listen to what man's wisdom tells us: we should listen to what the Holy Ghost who lives down in our belly teaches. I once asked a woman in a First Baptist Church, "Is the Holy Ghost in your belly?"

"Heavens no!" she exclaimed.

21

I said, "Well, the Lord told me to ask you that." She had been going to church for 28 years, and she was all "goofed up."

She said, "Hauh?"

I asked her again, "Don't you know if the Holy Ghost is in your belly or not?"

She said, "NO! I don't know if He is or not."

I said, "Well, He is not in there, then."

She said, "I have been going to church for twenty-eight years!"

I said, "What does that have to do with the Holy Ghost? You can go to church for fifty years. I just want to know: do you know for sure that the Holy Ghost is in your belly?"

She said again, "I don't know if He is or not."

I said, "He is not in there then. He is too strong, stout, and beautiful: too lovely and wonderful for you to not even know it." Then I asked her, "Do you want Him in there?"

She said, "Well, yeah."

Then I answered, "You have come to the right place." And she got Him in there that day!

"But the natural man receiveth not the things of the Spirit of God: for they are foolishness unto him: neither can he know them, because they are spiritually discerned" (v. 14).

If you would ask a person if the Holy Ghost is in his belly, he would think that was foolishness. The natural man cannot receive the things of the Spirit of God. He cannot discern them, because they are not naturally discerned.

You can't have *the word of wisdom* working for you unless you are *born again. You need to be born again, and baptized with the Holy Ghost.* People who live in sin obey the devil. They do not operate *the gifts of the Spirit.*

"But he that is spiritual judgeth all things, yet he himself is judged of no man. For who hath known the mind of the Lord, that he may instruct him? But we have the mind of Christ" (vv. 15, 16).

If you have the mind of the Lord, you are not going to make any mistakes. I can look back on my past and there were a lot of things in which I did not have the mind of Christ. I just did it on my own, just as you. You did it from the natural standpoint; just because you wanted to do it.

We just read that the natural man doesn't understand the things of God. You cannot understand God's will for you in your life, as long as you are in the natural. Unless you pray and read the Bible, you cannot know the will of God. You may belong to a church, but if you never read the Bible, and never pray, and somebody came and knocked on your door, and said, "God told me to tell you this: . . ." you would not accept it. Why?

Because you would think that it was foolishness. Get in the Word of God. Pray. Then if somebody comes to give you *a word of wisdom,* about what is to come to pass in your life, you can accept it. You will understand that the Holy Ghost is telling you something, through that person, that is going to happen to you in the future. And you need *that gift of the word of wisdom.* He may choose to send you some place to tell somebody the truth.

This gift is very important in your life. *A word of God's wisdom,* imparted unto you (the knowledge of God), will save you from making a bunch of *dumb mistakes* and

23

falling into *valleys and ditches.* It is very important for you to allow this gift to operate through you. Claim it.

A lot of Christians do not understand this, and they will say, "Well, Brother Norvel, how do I get these gifts?"

Claim them. Just as you do when you claim a healing. Say, "Thank you, Jesus. The 12th chapter of 1 Corinthians is mine. Thank you, Lord, for *the word of wisdom.* It is mine. Thank you, Lord, for *the gifts of healing.* It is mine." He will give you a *word of wisdom,* today: NOW.

These things are given to you as the Spirit wills. Because verse 7 says, "But the manifestation of the Spirit is given to every man to profit withal." That is getting back to the basic foundation of the gifts of the Spirit: where God listed those to the church. And as you can plainly read, God will not have you ignorant of these *gifts of the Spirit.* If you are ignorant of them you will not have them, because the Holy Ghost will try to operate and give some of them to you, and you won't even know what to do.

You will think, "Is that the Lord? I feel like the Lord is trying to show me something . . . ." Your body may be trembling, and tears running down your cheeks, and the Holy Ghost in you is beginning to move. Something funny sometimes starts happening inside of you. Well, you had better listen to what He is saying. He may be shaking you to tell you something. And it may be for your own benefit. Or He may do it just to see if you are a true believer in the Lord Jesus Christ, and that you are willing to pay the price to get the gospel out. He may tell you to go to another city and tell somebody what is going to happen to them in the future, at your own expense.

You need *the word of God's wisdom.*

7

God Gave Me A Vision

Many people have asked me, "Why does a businessman like you, who has eight or ten businesses, and all of them are making you a profit, fool around with a bunch of kids? Why are you going to college campuses, spending money, and giving out tracts and books?"

Well, I had no earthly idea that I was going to do it. It started about five years ago (at the time of this writing), when God gave me a vision.

Now, please do not misunderstand, and don't say after you read this book that I said that your dreams will come true. No! God has worked in some strange ways down through the history of the Bible, for human beings, to try to get them to do His will, and to show them things. We have already seen that He talked to men like Noah, and Paul. And He has gotten His knowledge across to individuals through dreams and visions. But you can't go around saying, "I am going to follow God through dreams." God has used His angels to get His *word of wisdom* across to the people. But again, you shouldn't just sit there and wait until an angel appears unto you.

It is important for you to know that God works through you by the Holy Ghost who lives on the inside of you. He will teach you all the truth, and He gives the *gifts of the Spirit* to get those truths to you.

A few years ago, they were having a meeting at Howard University in Washington, D.C. The Lord said for me to go to that meeting. I packed my clothes and caught a plane, and went to the Washington, D.C. airport. I had no idea that I was going to get *a word of God's wisdom* about what is going to come upon the earth in the future.

Howard University is where they were having the riots, back in the "Berkley days." That was when the kids would pile up hundreds of chairs in front of the gates, and do all kinds of dumb things. They were having riots on just about every campus across the country. Howard University was a *kind of toughy*—you know. But I went in there and said, "Here I am. The Lord sent me in here."

I met the University chaplain, and he said, "I've got three different places where you can stay." He started naming them off. One was a home of a Catholic priest.

I said, "Well, I might as well stay with a priest! Praise God forever!" They took me down to the house and there were about six Catholic priests in the place. I met them all, and they took me upstairs to the bedroom. I was there at the wishes of the conference. They were cooperating with the conference.

I shall never forget when one priest said, "Now right here, Mr. Hayes, is your bed. It hasn't been very long ago when a priest died in this bed." That was a nice thought you know! I'd like to go to heaven anyway! Is that the death bed?

A WORD OF WISDOM FROM GOD

When the priest left, I knelt down beside that bed, as I said, "Well, I guess I had better pray." All of a sudden, while I was praying, the Spirit of the Lord, showed me, *the word of God's wisdom.* He showed me what He wanted me to do in the future.

He said, "I want you to buy a school bus." Now remember—I was in Washington, D.C., in a Catholic priest's home, kneeling down by that "death bed!" praying. And the Holy Ghost showed me that He wanted me to buy a school bus for a certain pastor, who was over 700 miles away. He plainly showed me that *it would come to pass in the future.*

I said, "Okay: I will buy the school bus."

I want to teach you something right here. I will teach you the honesty of God, and how much you can trust Him. What was I supposed to do? If I didn't have any of God's wisdom, I might have just run out of there, bought a bus, jumped in it, and driven it 700 miles to the church where the Lord wanted me to give the bus. I just said, "Okay, Lord, I will buy the bus" (God wanted it to be done in the future, you know.): and I went on about my business.

Lucille Ball, Pat Boone, and others were supposed to be at the meeting, but they got all fouled up, somehow, and some showed up, and some didn't make it. Pat Boone was supposed to speak in the afternoon, but he didn't make it, and they asked me to speak. I wasn't supposed to be on the program; nevertheless, there I was sitting on the platform of Howard University, in front of a *packed out room* of people. They were standing around the walls.

The *How Are You? Boys* were singing a special, and they were going to introduce me as soon as they finished singing. All of a sudden, *the Spirit of prophecy* came upon me, in the form of a vision. As I sat there on the stage, I was getting a message down in my belly. The Holy Ghost can give you a message down there when it is *prophecy in known words. Prophecy* is "words in a known language, that you can understand, flowing out of your innermost being, and building the congregation up." I began to get a prophecy for that particular congregation.

Just remember: **if it is from God, and His Spirit comes on you to do something in a public service, you can hold it.** If it is not the Lord, you can't hold it. I have sat on platforms for over an hour, with the Spirit of prophecy just rolling on the inside of me; waiting for the first blank spot to come, so I could give it out. If it is from God, you will sit still and wait. It won't leave. You must wait upon the Lord, and for the right time.

(I saw in that vision, what was going to happen to the earth, spiritually. Now, I didn't see everything that is going to happen to the earth—spiritually. And I did not know, at that time, why God showed me the vision. It wasn't until two years later when my campus ministry started, that I began to see it. God showed me, because He wanted me involved. He has given several other people the same vision.)

That day at Howard University, I was just sitting there, and streams of tears were running down my cheeks: it was so sweet. The Spirit of prophecy was still in me when the singers were finished. I stood up and gave out the prophecy. God told that University Board something in that prophecy.

You may say, "Well, dear me, why were they having a meeting at Howard University when they were having riots?"

It is hard for the natural mind to perceive. There were so many riots on campus, and so many students who were so ruthless. But two of those boys on that campus got saved, and they had a burden for that campus. They were so filled with the Holy Ghost, that they talked the officials into giving them a check for $2,000., to have *a Holy Ghost meeting*. They said, "If you give us the money, we will have *a Holy Ghost meeting*, and we will change this campus."

As far as I know, that has never been done in the history of the world before. Imagine, taking $2,000. out of a college treasury in order to have *a Holy Ghost meeting*!

You may say, "Oh sure! You just go to Georgia Tech, and try to get that across to the dean."

That's all right! You let the Georgia Tech students pile the chairs down by the gates, down by the stadium, on campus for four or five times, then let them have to hire them to take the chairs back in, and they will start listening. It is like somebody who is dying with cancer, and they do not believe in healing, or that it is for them. Then they find that they are dying, with no hope. When this happens some of them will believe anything. Some of them will just go ahead and die. But some will be open for anything.

Now please read this very carefully. The sad part is, when they get ready to believe anything, they are usually so far that they can never get out of it, and they just die anyway. They have wasted their lives. They didn't read the Bible, therefore they don't have the healing verses on the inside of them. So when the cancer came and fastened itself upon their body, they had nothing to get them out of it: no power: no authority; nothing to make the cancer leave.

This is what you must understand about the devil, and the things that he tries to do to you. YOU have to make them leave in Jesus' name. YOU—not somebody else.

A lot of people are just waiting around to see if God will heal them *sometime*. Well, *you* make it leave, yourself, in Jesus' name. *You* claim the Scriptures and make the devil leave you alone. *You* stand steadfast in God's Word. The devil cannot pass over God's Word. Just quote Scripture to him, and you are just as safe as if you were in your mother's arms.

If you get God's Word inside you, and you quote Scripture to the devil, then when God gives you *a word of wisdom*, you will find that that is exactly the way it will be.

ANOTHER VISION THE LORD GAVE ME IN THE SPIRIT

Some years ago, God showed me another vision. I saw it in the spirit. In the Spirit, way up in the sky, I saw a big shoot of wind, like a whirlwind. It was coming straight out through the air, and then I saw another one. I looked over here, and I saw another. I looked over the other way, and I saw another. Then I could see the world — the four corners of the world — and that wind was like a whirlwind, coming from all four corners. The whirlwinds were coming towards each other, and they were about to meet head-on, and they did meet—right head-on—in the sky! When they did meet, all of the whirlwinds turned into one huge chute, as one; coming down to the earth, down, down, down to the earth. That was God's healing power for the human race: God's healing power for bodies; and God's healing power for salvation. There is something about the wind, that God just works through. The Spirit of God is coming like that wind. You don't know where it comes from but it is there. The wind starts going, but where does it come from? It is like a mystery.

"But we speak the wisdom of God in a mystery, even the hidden wisdom, which God ordained before the world unto our glory" (1 Corinthians 2:7).

The word of wisdom is like a mystery: the deep things of God are like a mystery to you. As you sit in your chair, reading this book, you may receive something from God. Or you may be riding in your car, and receive *a word of wisdom*. One manifestation of the Holy Ghost may not last over 30 seconds. The Spirit of God may show you something. But if you don't pray about it; walk softly, you could miss God, and it would cause you all kinds of trouble. He can show you the same thing about a business.

That day, on the stage, God said to me, "This is the way, son, that the revival is coming to the earth; coming to the earth . . . . Revival is coming to the earth. But it is going to come in the future—in the future. It is going to come mainly among the young people. I didn't say, 'totally;' I said, 'mainly among the young people.' "

The rest of the team members do not have the same vision that God gave me. Because the Lord showed me some years ago, how it was going to come. And the only way that they will have the same vision, is for God to give it to them supernaturally.

The revival is coming on the college campuses. Just get that through your head. I'm not talking about passing out tracts, or giving out *Cross and Switchblade* books to fraternities, and sororities, or in dormitories. I'm not talking about talking to a few students today, and a few students tomorrow. I am telling you, revival is coming to the college campuses in this country. You may as well get ready!

You may ask, "Well, when will it come?"

I don't know anything about that. God may have me passing out tracts, and giving out books, and doing this and that five years from now. I do not know *when, but mark it down—revival is coming.*

You may be attending a meeting, and it will be twenty times as big on the campus of the University of Georgia: on Georgia Tech. Jesus will be baptizing students with the Holy Ghost, all over the place. He will be healing them, and meeting all their needs. You will start hearing about it happening on different campuses.

We are only getting a little taste of it right now, but I can see it! It is like the springs; like the water falling: it is like the dew dripping down. A prayer group here, a prayer group there, a prayer group on different college campuses. It is coming. I know. Because God gave me a vision *of the word of wisdom;* it is going to happen in the future!

8

Stand Steadfast

The word of wisdom is a gift that is given to you by the Holy Spirit. It is a gift to *the Church—the Body of Christ,* and you are entitled to it. When it comes to you, *stand steadfast,* just as you do for a healing, and it will come to pass.

The *gift of the word of wisdom* may come to you quickly: it may be a few days; it may be a few weeks; it may take months, or possibly a few years. But you can know this, when *the word of wisdom* is imparted to you, by the Holy Spirit, He is showing you something that is going to take place in the future. God wants you to have the wisdom, in order to handle it.

Many Christians make the mistake of trying to rush God into doing things. God has His own timing.

It was about six or seven months after my stay in the Catholic priest's home, when God had told me to buy a certain pastor a school bus, and Dr. Lester Sumrall called and asked me to come and hold a meeting for him, in South Bend, Indiana. I agreed to do this, and a few months later, I went to South Bend.

Dr. Sumrall took me upstairs in his own house to a room. He told me that this was where I was going to stay. He told me to make myself at home, and that the people were going to enjoy my being there, and he asked me to let him know if I needed anything.

After Dr. Sumrall left me alone in the room, I felt a chill. (When I stay in someone's home, I always kneel down and ask God to bless that home, and all the people in it. I also ask the Lord if He wants to reveal anything to me, for them, that will encourage and bless them. And I tell Him that I will do it. I always want it to be from the Lord. I don't want to get mixed up in family problems. I always pray, "If anybody is going to get messed-up in the future, just feel free to use me, Lord: I am available." There have been many times when God would show me something, and I have walked up to one of the mates and told them what God said. They would begin to cry. I have said, "Now listen, you are not being fair to your husband. The Spirit of God wants me to talk to you . . . ." I haven't had a single person yet, who hasn't accepted what the Lord gave me through a word of wisdom, for them.)

As I knelt down and prayed, "God, bless Brother Summerall. Bless his home, and bless the people here, Jesus. And Lord, just make me a blessing while I am here." As I was praying, a word of the Lord came to me, saying, "I want you to buy that pastor a school bus."

I said, "Yes, I know You do. You told me eight or ten months ago that You wanted me to buy that school bus, when I was in Washington, D.C., in that Catholic Priest's home, kneeling by that 'death bed.' I remember what You told me. Jesus, I don't know what school bus that you want me to buy, and I can't be more honest with You. I am willing to buy that school bus, but I am also going to tell You, that I am not going to buy a school bus until You tell me what school bus that You want me to buy. When You show me what school bus You want me to buy, then I will buy it . . . . I might go ahead and buy a used school bus, and You wanted me to buy a new one. Or I might go out and buy a new one, when You want me to buy a used one. You show me what kind of school bus You want me to buy, and I will buy it. Thank You Lord."

Let us learn this about God: He respects honesty.

I owned the Yellow Cab Company, in the city where I live. And I used to get on my knees and pray, "Oh Lord, help me sell this flaky company. I don't want the Yellow Cab Company. Do You hear me? Please send me a buyer."

He did not send a buyer. I called all the drivers in (There were about eight or ten drivers.), when I first bought the company, and said, "Now listen, men. I don't fool around with girls, prostitutes, and whiskey. I know that is how a lot of you guys make your living. I don't make money that way. I don't make my money, crooked. The first driver that I find fooling with girls, or whiskey, I am going to fire you. I am not going to tell you twice. I am telling you right now, and that is it. SO—if that is what you are doing on the side, I am warning you right now, you had better stop it. Don't think that because you got away with it in the past that you can trick me. You may trick me for a while, but I will catch you. The Holy Ghost will show me."

I caught one of them, and I fired him. I think that I liked him best. I kept the company for eight years, and had 24-hour service, 7-days a week. I wanted to stop Sunday service, but many elderly people needed cabs to get to church. I decided that if I stopped this *flaky company* from Sunday service, those people couldn't get to church. Finally, I decided to close down on Sunday afternoons, after church. That was hard to do. Cab companies are important to a city. The mayor and the city council wanted it to operate 24-hours a day, 7-days a week, for emergencies and the like. You may go for ten years, and never need a cab, then suddenly at three o'clock in the morning you will need one.

It is always a good thing to have a taxi-cab company in a city. There was another cab company in town, and we went into partnership together. The other owner was an ex-sheriff of the town. One day, as time went on, we discussed dissolving partnership. I said that we could do it on a give and take basis. He drew up a contract that said that he would pay me so much, and I couldn't start another cab company in Cleveland, Tennessee for ten years. I signed the contract, he paid me the amount that we had agreed on, and I went down to the bank to deposit the money.

Now, it was God's time!

As I stepped up to the teller's window, I saw the pastor that God had told me to buy a school bus for. I said, "Hi! Pastor."

He stepped over to me and said, "Where in the world have you been, Brother Norvel? Where has the Good Lord taken you since the last time I saw you?"

I said, "All over."

He said, "I don't doubt that!"

"Well — uh . . . ."

He interrupted, "You know, I was down the highway, and I was going to see the banker tomorrow, when all of a sudden, the Spirit of the Lord came upon me, and told me to go to the bank this afternoon. So I got into my car and came up here."

I said, "What did you come up here for?"

He said, "Cleveland State College is over here, and they have a school bus that they want to sell. They are taking bids on it. The highest bidder will get the bus. I just put in a bid, and when they opened up the box, where the bids were placed, my envelope was the only one in there."

36

By this time, the Holy Ghost was just causing my insides to jump up and down, saying, "This is the bus! This is the bus!"

I remembered my prayer in Lester Sumrall's bedroom, when I said, "Now Jesus, I am not going to buy a bus until You show me the one that You want me to buy, and I will buy it, You know."

I heard the Lord now telling me, "That is what you said."

I said, "Yes, Lord, You are right."

I turned to the pastor and said, "Well, Pastor! Glory to God. I am glad to get this off my mind!"

He said, "Huh?"

I said, "I am glad to get this off of me."

"Get what off of you?" he asked.

I said, "The bus . . . the bus! You wouldn't understand, Pastor. But you don't have to see any banker. Just trust me."

Of course he knew me real well. We had been together many times before. He said, "I won't do anything until you tell me what you want me to do."

I said, "Come get into my car and we will go to my office." We arrived at my office and I told my secretary to write the pastor out a check for the amount of the bus.

God had given me *a word of wisdom* many months before. Something was *to be done in the future.* And that was the time for it to come to pass.

"For to one is given by the Spirit the word of wisdom . . . ." (1 Corinthians 12:8).

Has the Spirit of God been dealing with you and you didn't even know what it was?

I can tell you right now what it is—it's a word of wisdom from God if He's showing you something that's going to come to pass in the future. It's a word of God's knowledge for you—to let you know. And you're involved in it. You might as well get ready.

If God has shown you something, but you didn't know what it was until now, and you want to yield yourself to God and say, "I'll do it," tell Him.

Say: "Jesus, I believe in the gifts of the Spirit. I believe in the word of wisdom. I believe the word of wisdom is a word of God's knowledge coming to me and letting me know something that God wants to come to pass.

"I ask you Jesus to help me.

"I remember that thing that the Lord's been dealing with me about. I remember, Jesus, when you spoke it to me. I give myself to You, totally. I am available to carry that out, any time you want to bring it to pass.

"Thank you, Lord, for giving me a word of wisdom so that I won't be deceived, but I can go and carry out the work that the Spirit of God wants me to carry out.

"I love you Jesus. I praise you Jesus. I love the 12th chapter of I Corinthians. I thank you for the gifts of the Spirit given to me as the Spirit wills. Thank you, Lord."